11+
Maths

TESTBOOK **2**

Numerical Reasoning
Standard 15 Minute Tests

Dr Stephen C Curran

Edited by Katrina MacKay

This book belongs to

ae
PUBLICATIONS

Accelerated Education Publications Ltd

Do your workings on this page

Mark to %	
0	0%
1	7%
2	13%
3	20%
4	27%
5	33%
6	40%
7	47%
8	53%
9	60%
10	67%
11	73%
12	80%
13	87%
14	93%
15	100%

Maths Test 1

1) How many months have exactly **30** days? _4_

2) Reduce **6.38** by **twenty-nine hundredths**. _6·09_

3) What is the sum of the following numbers that are divisible by **6**? _300_

   60 216 27 84

4) What is the next number in the sequence?

   1, 5, 10, 16, _23_

5) The diagram shows the first three square numbers. What is the **5th** square number? _25_

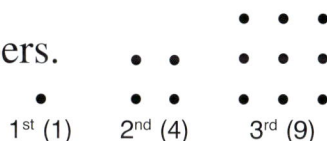

   1st (1)   2nd (4)   3rd (9)

6) The floor and ceiling of this room are _horizontal_ .

   (horizontal, vertical, diagonal)

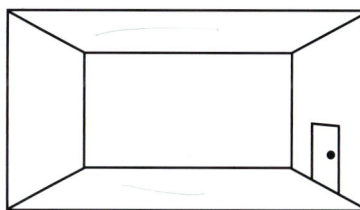

7) What is the largest number that is a factor of **64** and **80**? _8 16_

8) Add the sum of **4** and **6** to the product of **4** and **6**. _34_

9) List all the factors of **24**.

   _1,2,3,4,6,8,12,24_

10) What is the average of **1.25**, **3.25** and **6.0**? _3·5_

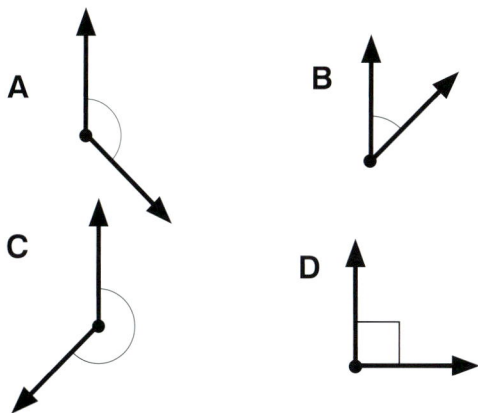

A   B   C   D

11) Which is a right angle? _D_

12) Which is an acute angle? _B_

13) Convert **256** hours to days and hours. _10days 16h_

14) Subtract **2.8** from $4\frac{1}{4}$. ___

15) What is the next number in the sequence?

   108, 95, 82, _69_

Score [ ]   Percentage [%]

© 2016 Stephen Curran

3

Do your workings on this page

Mark to %	
0	0%
1	7%
2	13%
3	20%
4	27%
5	33%
6	40%
7	47%
8	53%
9	60%
10	67%
11	73%
12	80%
13	87%
14	93%
15	100%

Maths Test 2

This magic square adds up to the same amount in all directions.

A		20
	15	B
10	15	

1) What is the value of **A**? _10_

2) What is the value of **B**? _5_

---

3) **1996** was a leap year. Will **2046** be a leap year? _no_

4) What is the next fraction?

$\frac{1}{2}, \frac{1}{6}, \frac{1}{18},$ _1/54_

---

5) List the factors of **48**.

_1, 2, 3, 4, 6, 8, 12, 16, 24, 48_

6) What is the average of **24**, **32**, **15** and **17**? _22_

---

7) There are **90** degrees in a right angle. How many degrees are there in one and a half turns of a circle? _540°_

---

8) This magic square adds up to the same amount horizontally and vertically.

What is the value of **A**? _19_

	A	
10		17
13	8	9

9) $(40 \div 8) \times 4 =$ _20_

10) Deduct **4 tenths** from **1.36**.
_0·96_

11) What is the sum of the even numbers between **27** and **35**?
_124_

---

12) Pippa is not as tall as Priya. Amber is not as short as Priya. Who is the tallest? _Amba_

13) Eoghan starts facing west. He turns anticlockwise to face north. How many right angles has he passed through? _3_

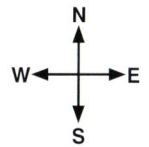

---

14) What fraction of this shape is shaded?

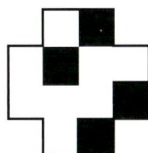

_1/3_

15) If **6** is subtracted from $\frac{1}{4}$ of the original number the answer is **12**. What is the original number?
_72_

Score [ ] Percentage [ ] %

Do your workings on this page

Maths Test 3

1) What is the sum of the odd numbers between **72** and **82**?
_385_

2) What is the value of x? _28_

$$x + 16 = 4(5 + 6)$$

3) What is the value of the **7** in **3.947**? _7 thouthasdnths_

4) Harry is taller than Talvir but shorter than Shereen. Shereen is taller than Max. Who is the tallest? _Shereen_

5) **16.5 − 21.9** = _−5.4_

6) How many days are there from the **24th** of September to the **12th** of November (include both days)? _50_

7) Is **45** a triangular number?
yes
_4 − 80_

8) **One** bottle holds **7** cups of juice. How many bottles are needed if **149** people have **2** cups each? _42_

9) **4.73 + 0.7 + 0.043** = _5.473_
_5.430t_

10) What is the average of **17, 21, 8, 9** and **32**? _17.4_

In what ratio are the:

11)

black and white marbles?

(B : W)

_5.8_

12)

Die A   Die B

visible spots on the dice?

(A : B)

_14/7=2:1_

13)

Domino A   Domino B

total number of spots on each domino?

(A : B)

_7.6_

14) Timmy's watch is **4** minutes fast. At what time on his watch must he start his **13** minute journey to the train station if the train leaves at **8.45am** but he wants to arrive **5** minutes early? _8.31_

15) How many right angles are in the letters below? _13_

A F H T M E

Score ☐ Percentage ☐ %

Do your workings on this page

© 2016 Stephen Curran

Mark to %	
0	0%
1	7%
2	13%
3	20%
4	27%
5	33%
6	40%
7	47%
8	53%
9	60%
10	67%
11	73%
12	80%
13	87%
14	93%
15	100%

Maths Test 4

1) **Three** out of every **seven** pens in a pencil case are red. The rest are blue. If there are **35** pens in the pencil case, how many are blue? _20_

2) $\frac{12}{16} = \frac{?}{4}$ _3_

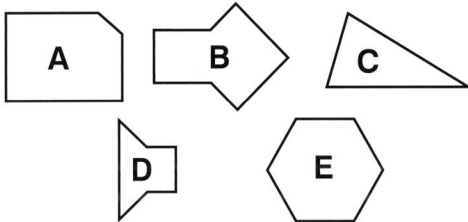

A B C

3) Which shape is a regular polygon? _E_

D E

4) Which shape is a heptagon? _B_

5) If Aron was **four** times his present age he would be **five** years older than his mother who is **43**. How old is Aron? _12_

6) Mary's grandfather turned **85** in **2013**. In what year was he born? _1928_

7) $3x - 6 = x + 4$

What is the value of x? _5_

8) How many degrees are there in $\frac{1}{4}$ of a right angle? _22·5_

9) Draw a dot pattern to show that **10** is a rectangular number.

10) $30n = 120$

What is the value of n? _4_

11) Deduct **2.32** from **8.28**. _5·96_

12) $\frac{12}{32} = \frac{36}{?}$ _96_

13) **£5.00** was shared between **8** girls and **14** boys. If each girl received **31p** and the remaining money was shared equally between the boys, how much did each boy get? _18p_

14) Take **0.06** from **0.64**. _0·58_

15) How many days are there from the **11th** of March to the **4th** of May (include both days)? _55_

Score ☐ Percentage ☐ %

Do your workings on this page

Mark to %	
0	0%
1	7%
2	13%
3	20%
4	27%
5	33%
6	40%
7	47%
8	53%
9	60%
10	67%
11	73%
12	80%
13	87%
14	93%
15	100%

Maths Test 5

1) Find the sum of the prime numbers between **38** and **64**. _304_

2) What are the next numbers in the sequence?
23, **27**, **32**, _38_ , _45_

3) Which is a reflex angle? _C_

A B C D

4) If **130** cartons fit in **1** box, how many boxes would be needed to store **800** cartons? _7_

5) What is the difference between the average and the range of **17**, **15** and **22**? _11_

6) When a number is multiplied by itself and **15** is added to it the answer is **159**. What is the number? _12_

7) Write $\frac{3}{100}$ as a decimal. _0·03_

8) $8 - 6 - 1 = 8 - (5 - 2)$
Is this true? _No_

9) $60 \div 4 =$ _75_ $\div 5$

10) Write **0.007** as a fraction. _$\frac{7}{1000}$_

11) There are **12** sweets in a bag and a box holds **16** bags. If Andrew buys **6** friends **50** sweets each, how many boxes would he have to buy? _2_

12) Ryan can write **14** lines in **5** minutes. How many lines can he write in **2** hours? _336_

13) How many sides does a heptagon have? _7_

14) Which is an obtuse angle? _D_

A B C D

15) How many minutes are there in a week? _10 080_

Score [ ] Percentage [ ] %

Do your workings on this page

Mark to %	
0	0%
1	7%
2	13%
3	20%
4	27%
5	33%
6	40%
7	47%
8	53%
9	60%
10	67%
11	73%
12	80%
13	87%
14	93%
15	100%

Maths Test 6

1) What is the next number in the sequence? **1, 4, 9, 16,** _____

2) Reduce **3.725** by **1.75**. _____

3) How many minutes are there in $12\frac{1}{10}$ hours? _____

4) Matthew's grandmother turned **88** in **2012**. In which year was she born? _____

5) This magic square adds up to **57** in all directions. What are the values of **A** and **B**?

A = _____

B = _____

	15	20
	19	A
18	B	

6) What fraction of **1,000** is **125**? _____

7) Write all the factors of **36**.

_____

8) What is the missing number?
62, 46, _____, 14

9) What is the **seventh** triangular number? _____

1st ● (1)
2nd ●● (3)
3rd ●●● (6)

10) Take $\frac{3}{4}$ from **0.9**. _____

11) How many seconds are there in $1\frac{1}{6}$ hours? _____

12) $\frac{1}{3}$ of a number is **8**. What is $\frac{3}{4}$ of this number? _____

13) What is the average of **6.0**, **7.5** and **13.5**? _____

14) On what day will the **18th** of August be? _____

JULY						
Sun	Mon	Tue	Wed	Thu	Fri	Sat
			1	2	3	4
5	6	7	8	9	10	11

15) When a number is multiplied by **7** and **24** is added to it the answer is **269**. What is this number?

_____

Score [   ] Percentage [%]

Do your workings on this page

Mark to %	
0	0%
1	7%
2	13%
3	20%
4	27%
5	33%
6	40%
7	47%
8	53%
9	60%
10	67%
11	73%
12	80%
13	87%
14	93%
15	100%

Maths Test 7

1) Insert a decimal point in **278496** so the **9** has a value of **9 thousandths**. _____

2) Which of these numbers is both rectangular and triangular? _____
16   55   27   37

3) Which is a reflex angle? _____
90°   136°   15°   237°

4) $28.257 \times 100 =$ _____

5) How many days are there altogether in March, April and May? _____

6) What is the value of the **7** in **28.6753**?
_____

7) Put in order of size, smallest first:
6.85   6$\frac{5}{6}$ 6$\frac{4}{5}$ _____

8) $15\overline{)3957}$ = _____

9) There are **24** sweets in a packet. **8** are cherry, **12** are lemon and the rest are orange. If Hilde closes her eyes and picks a sweet at random, what is the probability that the sweet is orange? _____

10) In a class of **32** students, **14** walk to school and the rest travel by car. What is the simplest ratio of students who walk to school to students who travel by car? _____

11) A hockey match started at **2.00pm** and lasted **75** minutes. If there were **22** minutes added for half time and **6** additional minutes of injury time, at what time did the match finish? _____

12) $81.7 \times 100 =$
_____

13) **20** sweets were shared between friends. Toni received **25%**, Alex received $\frac{1}{5}$ and Taran was given the rest. How many did Taran recieve? _____

14) A darts player threw **3** darts. She hit **12** on her first throw, **double 16** on her second and **triple 8** on her third. What was her total score? _____

15) The news started at **10.20pm** and finished **75** minutes later. At what time did it finish? _____

Score [   ]   Percentage [%]

Do your workings on this page

Mark to %	
0	0%
1	7%
2	13%
3	20%
4	27%
5	33%
6	40%
7	47%
8	53%
9	60%
10	67%
11	73%
12	80%
13	87%
14	93%
15	100%

Maths Test 8

1) What is the next number in the sequence? **5, 7, 11, 17,** ____

2) What is the sum of **six tenths** and **four hundredths**? _____

3) What date was the first day of **2014**? Write in figures. _____

4) $\dfrac{1}{4} = \dfrac{8}{?}$ _____

5) What are the factors of **28**? _____

6) There are **ten** years in a decade. How many decades are there in a century? _____

7) Boxes of books are packed with **8** books per box. How many boxes are needed for **104** books? _____

8) The **fourth** triangular number is **10**. What is the **eighth** triangular number? _____

9) What is the mean of **16, 27, 13, 12** and **22**? _____

10) What are the common factors of **18** and **24**? _____

11) Reduce **twenty thousand** by **eight**. Give your answer in figures. _____

12) A number is multiplied by itself, then by the original number. The answer is **125**. What was the original number? _____

13) What number is halfway between **14** and **30**? _____

14) Which is an acute angle? ____   15) Which is an obtuse angle? ____

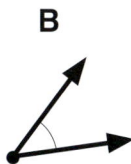

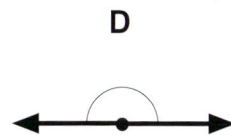

A   B   C   D

Score [   ]   Percentage [   ] %

Do your workings on this page

Mark to %	
0	0%
1	7%
2	13%
3	20%
4	27%
5	33%
6	40%
7	47%
8	53%
9	60%
10	67%
11	73%
12	80%
13	87%
14	93%
15	100%

Maths Test 9

1) How many right angles are there in $1\frac{5}{8}$ of a full rotation? _____

2) $0.67 + 925 + 1.302 =$

   _____

3) Which of these are square numbers?

   144 53 49 101 12 _____

4) $16\overline{)432}$ = _____

5) What is the mean of
   6, 17, 28 and **39**? _____

6) If George were **seven** times his present age, he would be **four** years younger than his mother, who is **32**. How old is George? _____

7) What is the highest common factor of **156** and **182**? _____

8) Write the missing numbers in this series.
   ___, **57**, **43**, ___, **18**, **7**

9) What is $\frac{5}{7}$ of **126**?

   _____

10) A petting zoo has **15** puppies, **9** kittens and **18** bunnies.
    What is the ratio of puppies to kittens to bunnies? _____

11) Oliver practises guitar for $\frac{1}{15}$ of a day, **five** days a week.
    How many hours does he practise in a week? _____

12) Express **21.79** in **hundredths**.
    _____ hundredths

13) $4\overline{)2.7}$ = _____
    (Answer to 2 d.p.)

14) What is the value of x? _____ $8x - 12 = 63 + 3x$

15) Jasper is at school from **7.30am** until **3.30pm**.
    What fraction of the day does he spend out of school? _____

Score ☐   Percentage ☐ %

Do your workings on this page

Mark to %	
0	0%
1	7%
2	13%
3	20%
4	27%
5	33%
6	40%
7	47%
8	53%
9	60%
10	67%
11	73%
12	80%
13	87%
14	93%
15	100%

Maths Test 10

1) **Twenty-five** is a square number.
   Which of these are square numbers? _____

   144 7 27 64 21

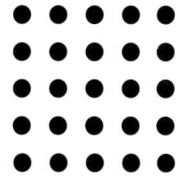

2) What is the average of
   $2\frac{1}{4}$, $4\frac{7}{12}$, $7\frac{2}{3}$ and $5\frac{1}{2}$? _____

3) Put in order of size, largest first:

   7.12 $7\frac{1}{9}$ 7.125 _____

4) What is the value of x? ____

   $6x + 17 = 5$

5) What must be subtracted from
   81 so that it will divide exactly
   into **four** groups of **17**? _____

6) $\frac{792}{66}$ = _____

7) $9\overline{)1863}$ = _____

8) A doctor is at her office from
   8am until **5.15pm**, **six** days a
   week. How many hours a week
   does she work?

   _____ hr(s) _____ min(s)

9) **196.68 ÷ 100 =** _____

10) $\frac{5}{25}$ is $\frac{1}{5}$ when simplified to
    its lowest terms. Write $\frac{32}{104}$ in
    its lowest terms. _____

11) Put in order of size, smallest first: $\frac{914}{100}$ **9.13% 0.915** _____

12) Which is an obtuse
    angle? _____

    189° 179° 29° 279°

13) The product of three numbers is **216**.
    Two of the numbers are **9** and **3**.
    What is the third number? _____

14) Ladders **A** and **B** are _____ to each other.
    (diagonal, horizontal, vertical, perpendicular, parallel)

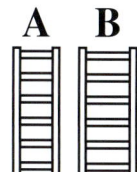

15) Benjamin's watch is **13** minutes slow. At what time on his watch
    must he start his **15** minute walk to the station to catch the
    9.38am train? _____

Score [ ] Percentage [%]

Do your workings on this page

Mark to %	
0	0%
1	7%
2	13%
3	20%
4	27%
5	33%
6	40%
7	47%
8	53%
9	60%
10	67%
11	73%
12	80%
13	87%
14	93%
15	100%

Maths Test 11

1) What are the factors of **29**? _____

2) Stefan will be **27** in July **2020**. How old was he in January **2000**? _____

3) What are the next two numbers in the sequence?
3, 15, 9, 45, ____, ____, **189**

4) How many rectangles can be seen? ____

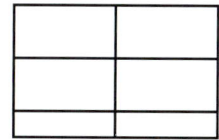

5) What is **246°** as a fraction of **360°**? _____

6) Fran has **60** marbles. The ratio of green to yellow marbles is **13 : 17**. How many yellow marbles are there? _____

7) Add the prime numbers between **12** and **20**. _____

8) Is **20** a triangular number? _____

9) $0.015 \times 36 =$ _____

10) Which numbers are not prime numbers?
29   38   102   51   91   _____

11) If a negative number is subtracted from a negative number does the value increase or decrease? _____

12) **Three** out of every **seven** children in a class are boys. If there are **28** children in the class, how many girls are there? _____

13) Over the weekend Ariel read a book. On Saturday she read **33** pages. On Sunday she read $\frac{1}{3}$ of the pages. She has $\frac{7}{15}$ of the book left to read. How many pages are in the book altogether? _____

14) $9^2 + 3^3 + 5^3 =$ _____

15) Which shapes have lines of symmetry? _____

A   B   C   D

Score [   ]   Percentage [   ] %

Do your workings on this page

Mark to %	
0	0%
1	7%
2	13%
3	20%
4	27%
5	33%
6	40%
7	47%
8	53%
9	60%
10	67%
11	73%
12	80%
13	87%
14	93%
15	100%

Maths Test 12

1) Which number is **5** times smaller than **two hundred and fifty thousand**? _____

2) What is **12³**? _____	3) $9^3 + 5^2 + 11^3 + 10^2 =$ _____
4) What are the missing numbers? **0, 1, 3, 6, ____, 19, ____**	5) $5^3 = 25 + 33 + 41 +$ _____
6) $21\overline{)11928}$ = _____	7) $\dfrac{4}{5} \times \dfrac{45}{80} =$ _____

8) Convert the mixed number $9\dfrac{5}{18}$ into an improper fraction. _____

9) Which is the largest? $\dfrac{1}{3}$ $\dfrac{17}{19}$ $\dfrac{7}{8}$ $\dfrac{4}{20}$ _____

10) Pawel's dad was born in **1967**. Pawel's mum is **five** years younger than his dad. In what year will Pawel's mum be **70** years old? _____

11) Which shape is not symmetrical? _____   A B C D

12) How many axes of symmetry does this circle have? _____ ○

13) What is the value of the **7** in **926.74**. _____

14) **Three** out of **ten** children have mobile phones. If **18** children have mobile phones, how many children are there altogether? _____

15) The **10.57am** train from Slough is **15** minutes late. Jasminder's watch is **7** minutes fast. What time does Jasminder's watch show when the train arrives? _____

Score [ ]   Percentage [%]

Do your workings on this page

Mark to %	
0	0%
1	7%
2	13%
3	20%
4	27%
5	33%
6	40%
7	47%
8	53%
9	60%
10	67%
11	73%
12	80%
13	87%
14	93%
15	100%

Maths Test 13

1) $9.015 \times 100 =$ _____

3) $6.72 \div 1.4 =$ _____

2) What fraction of a full rotation is $72°$? _____ $\frac{1}{6}$ $\frac{1}{5}$ $\frac{1}{4}$

4) What are the factors of **21**?

_____

5) Tayyib was **17** when his brother was born in **1995**.
When was Tayyib born? _____

6) What must be multiplied by **6** to get half of **684**? _____

7) Add the prime numbers between **28** and **38**. _____

8) $7x + 21 = 3x + 37$
What is the value of x? _____

9) The two triangular numbers **1** and **3** make the square number **4**.

Which two triangular numbers make this square number? _____

10) What are the next two numbers in the sequence?
8, **9**, **13**, **22**, _____, _____

11) **17** is a prime number.

A prime number has no other factors except itself and _____ .

12) **3** out of every **5** children in a class play football. If there are **40** children in a class, how many do not play football? _____

13) How many triangles can be seen? _____

14) Jo is at school from **8.30am** until **4.30pm**. In that time she does **6** hours of work. When Jo goes home she does **2** hours of work. What fraction of her day does she spend working?

_____

15) What is the value of the **6** in **18.456**? _____

Score [   ]   Percentage [**%**]

Do your workings on this page

Mark to %	
0	0%
1	7%
2	13%
3	20%
4	27%
5	33%
6	40%
7	47%
8	53%
9	60%
10	67%
11	73%
12	80%
13	87%
14	93%
15	100%

Maths Test 14

1) Which of the following numbers are multiples of **3** or **7**? _____

   9 19 56 158 168

2) Round **4.997** to 2 d.p.

   _____

3) A bakery makes **540** pies. It sells **297** pies. What fraction is unsold? _____

4)

   This is a plan for a garden.

   a) What is the perimeter of the garden. _____

   b) What is the area of the garden. _____

5) $? \longrightarrow \boxed{-\ 11 \div 18} \longrightarrow 31$ _____

6) $972 \longrightarrow \boxed{\div\ 6 - ?} \longrightarrow 75$ _____

7) $x + 4y = 3$

   $5x + 20y =$ _____

8) Which shape has a different perimeter from the others? _____

   12cm □ A   9cm ⬠ B   8cm ⬡ C   6cm ⯃ D   7cm ▭ E 17cm

9) The probability that it will snow on Christmas Day is **0.35**. What is the chance that it will not snow? _____

10) When it is **00:00** in London it is **08:00** in Kuala Lumpur, Malaysia. A plane leaves London at **13:45**. The journey takes **12** hours **25** minutes. In local time, when did it arrive in Kuala Lumpur? _____

11) Which of these fractions has the smallest value? _____ $\dfrac{2}{3}$ $\dfrac{5}{6}$ $\dfrac{4}{9}$ $\dfrac{13}{15}$ $\dfrac{9}{13}$

12) Adwoa works at a daycare centre. If she works from **8.40am** to **5.25pm**, **5** days a week, how many hours will she work in a **four-week** month? _____

13) $8^3 - (6^2 + 3^3) =$ ____

14) How many hours are there in total in May and June? _____

15) Use $+ - \times \div$ to complete the equation correctly:

   $6x - 15 = 8x$ ___ $(2x + 15)$

   Score ☐ Percentage ☐ %

Do your workings on this page

Mark to %	
0	0%
1	7%
2	13%
3	20%
4	27%
5	33%
6	40%
7	47%
8	53%
9	60%
10	67%
11	73%
12	80%
13	87%
14	93%
15	100%

Maths Test 15

1) What is the size of angle x? _____   153°

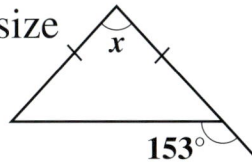

2) This net makes a box. What is the volume of the box? _____   2cm 3cm 6cm

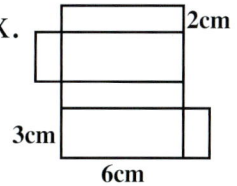

3) In a test Jacob scored **42** out of **70** marks. What percentage was incorrect? _____

4) What is the difference between **23°C** and **-5°C**? _____

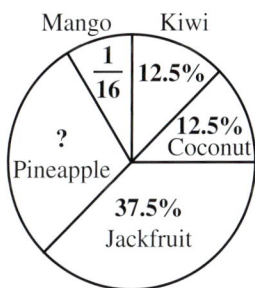

5) Several hundred people were asked their favourite fruit. **50** people like mangoes.

Mango Kiwi $\frac{1}{16}$ 12.5% 12.5% Coconut ? Pineapple 37.5% Jackfruit

a) How many people were questioned? _____

b) How many people like pineapples? _____

6) This magic square adds up to **81** in every direction. Find the value of **A** and **B**.

A = _____

B = _____

30	23	
	A	
	31	B

7) The sum of two numbers is **90**. Their difference is **14**. What are the numbers? _____

8) What is the sum of the internal angles in a regular pentagon? _____

9) _____$^2 - 24 = 145$

10) What is the next number in the sequence?
0.1, 0.01, 0.001, _____

11) What is the lowest common multiple of **4, 5** and **9**? _____

12) A number is squared, **12** is added, and it is divided by **4** to get **28**. What is the number? _____

13) **32 $\overline{)952}$** = _____

14) There are **six** teams playing volleyball: red, blue, green, yellow, purple, white. How many games are there if every team play each other once? _____

15) What fraction of the shape is shaded? _____

Score [ ]   Percentage [%]

Do your workings on this page

Mark to %	
0	0%
1	7%
2	13%
3	20%
4	27%
5	33%
6	40%
7	47%
8	53%
9	60%
10	67%
11	73%
12	80%
13	87%
14	93%
15	100%

Maths Test 16

1) What fraction of this shape is shaded? _____

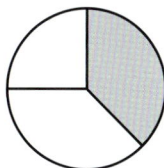

2) $10^6 =$ _____

3) $a = 10 \quad b = 12$

   $a^3 \div b^2 =$ _____ (1 d.p.)

4) What is **0.545** as a fraction?

   _____

5) Write $\frac{18}{30}$ as a percentage. _____

6) $26 \overline{)9865} =$ _____

   (Write your answer to 2 d.p.)

7) $3\frac{5}{6} - 2\frac{4}{5} =$ _____

8) What is the highest factor of **58** (excluding **58**)? _____

9) A multiple of **7** is any number that has **7** as a factor. Which of the following is not a multiple of **7**? _____

   63   105   49   43   119   35

10) A watch is **12** minutes slow and shows **9.06am**. Another watch is **15** minutes fast. What is the time on the second watch? _____

11) Brian is facing north-west. If he turns clockwise through an angle of **225°**, in what direction will he be facing? _____

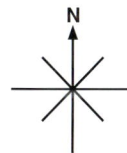

12) The _____ of a circle is half the length of the diameter. (circumference, radius, tangent, perimeter)

13) Anne sleeps from **8pm** until **7.30am**. What fraction of a day does she spend asleep? _____

14) **3** is a factor of **6**.
    3 is also a factor of **21**.
    3 is a common factor of **6** and **21**.
    Name two common factors of **12** and **36** (excluding **1**). _____

15) Jim has **£45**. He gives $\frac{1}{5}$ to his mum and $\frac{1}{3}$ to his dad. How much money does he have left? _____

Score [   ]   Percentage [   ] %

Do your workings on this page

Mark to %	
0	0%
1	7%
2	13%
3	20%
4	27%
5	33%
6	40%
7	47%
8	53%
9	60%
10	67%
11	73%
12	80%
13	87%
14	93%
15	100%

Maths Test 17

1) Sam is facing east. If he turns clockwise through three right angles, in what direction will he be facing? _____

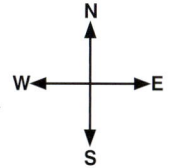

2) Find the average of **10.76**, **21.42** and **9.82**. _____

3) $\frac{18}{25} \div \frac{81}{5} =$ _____

4) $0.75 \times £18 =$ ____

5) $12^2 = 75 +$ _____

6) $(11 \times 8) + (12 \times 7) = 4 \times$ ____

7) Fill in the missing number in the sequence.

   2, 3, 11, 38, ____, 227

8) What fraction of a full rotation is **176°**? _____

9) Which two triangular numbers make this square number?

   _____ and _____

10) $21\overline{)9658} =$ _____

   (Write your answer as a decimal to 2 d.p.)

11) Trains leave Ealing Broadway station every **7** minutes. The first train leaves at **7.00am**. Bill arrives at Ealing Broadway at **8.05am**. What time is the next train that he can catch? _____

12) What is $\frac{9}{51}$ as a decimal to 2 d.p.? _____

13) **96** mints are shared among **16** boys and **24** girls. If each girl receives **2** sweets, how many does each boy receive? _____

14) What is the total of the odd numbers between **88** and **96**? _____

15) What is **20mm** of **40cm** as a fraction?

$\frac{5}{20}$ $\frac{6}{36}$ $\frac{1}{20}$ $\frac{1}{15}$ _____

Score [   ]   Percentage [   ] %

Do your workings on this page

Mark to %	
0	0%
1	7%
2	13%
3	20%
4	27%
5	33%
6	40%
7	47%
8	53%
9	60%
10	67%
11	73%
12	80%
13	87%
14	93%
15	100%

Maths Test 18

1) Which ratio is not the same as **6 : 13**? _____

   a $3 : 6\frac{1}{2}$ **b** $18 : 39$ **c** $2 : 4\frac{2}{3}$ **d** $9 : 19.5$ **e** $\frac{18}{3} : \frac{26}{2}$

---

2) Laura is on holiday. It costs her **7p** to send a text and **2p** to receive a text. If she receives **4** texts and sends **7** texts each day of her **5** day holiday, what is her total bill? _____

---

3) Buses leave a station every **7** minutes from **7.05am**. At what time does the **fifth** bus leave? _____

---

4) There are **250** CDs at a radio station. $\frac{2}{5}$ are rock music, **30%** are jazz, **15** are classical and the rest are pop. How many pop CDs are there? _____

---

5) $144 = 12 \times (3 + \underline{\quad})$ | 6) What is **35%** of **240**? _____

---

7) What is the name of this shape? _____
   (rhombus, trapezium, parallelogram)

---

8) $9^3 = \underline{\quad}$ | 9) What fraction of a complete rotation is **30°**? _____

---

10) How many more triangles must be shaded so that $\frac{40}{48}$ of the shape are shaded? _____

---

11) Charlie is using a map where **1cm** represents **3km**. He walks **18km**. How far is his walk on the map? _____

---

12) What is the sum of the square numbers between **6** and **52**? _____

Using the numbers: **13   16   14   13   12   21   13   18   24**

13) What is the median? _____

14) What is the mode? _____

15) What is the range? _____

Score [　　] Percentage [　　%]

Do your workings on this page

Mark to %	
0	0%
1	7%
2	13%
3	20%
4	27%
5	33%
6	40%
7	47%
8	53%
9	60%
10	67%
11	73%
12	80%
13	87%
14	93%
15	100%

Maths Test 19

1) Shadrak collected data from **70** children about their favourite subject. How many girls gave English as their favourite subject? _____

	Maths	English	Art
Boys	16	10	7
Girls	8	?	12

2) Marta usually buys a **200ml** coffee. She sees a coffee that is **35%** larger. What is the volume of the larger coffee? _____

3) What is the size of angle x in this isosceles triangle? _____

4) The area of a square is **16m²**. What is the perimeter of the square? _____

5) Which of these numbers is neither a square nor cube number? _____
1   12   16   64   169

6) The time in Athens is **2** hours ahead of the time in London. A flight takes **3** hours and **27** minutes. If the flight leaves London at **15:42**, at what local time does it arrive? _____

7) Which two lines are perpendicular? _____

A / B \
C —— D ——

8) How many prime numbers are there between **4** and **22**? _____

9) Amy is selling tickets to a theatre production. If she sells **84** tickets at **£7.40** each, how much money does she make?
_____

10) $6x + 5 = 3x + 17$
What is the value of x? ____

11) It takes a truck **2** days to travel **160km**. How long does it take to travel **400km**? _____

12) How many axes of symmetry does a regular heptagon have? _____

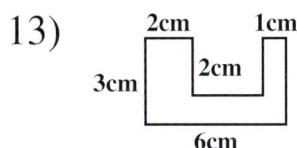

13) What is the: a) area of this shape? _____
b) perimeter of this shape? _____

14) James' father will be **four** times James' current age in **two** years. If James was **11** last year, how old is his father? _____

15) How many weeks are in a decade? ____

Score [   ]   Percentage [   ] %

ae © 2016 Stephen Curran

Do your workings on this page

Mark to %	
0	0%
1	7%
2	13%
3	20%
4	27%
5	33%
6	40%
7	47%
8	53%
9	60%
10	67%
11	73%
12	80%
13	87%
14	93%
15	100%

Maths Test 20

1) What is the size of angle x? _____

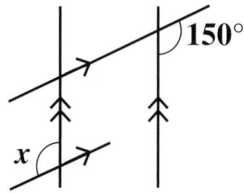

2) On what day was the **28th** of March? _____

MAY						
Sun	Mon	Tue	Wed	Thu	Fri	Sat
	1	2	3	4	5	6
7	8	9	10			

3) What is the sum of the first **5** prime numbers? _____

4) In a **20km** fun-run for charity, Katy runs **6** kilometres, jogs **55%** of the way and walks the rest. How far does she walk? _____

5) Which fraction can be used to make this equation correct? _____
$$\frac{3}{4} < \frac{4}{?} < \frac{5}{6}$$

6) A coach holds **51** people. How many coaches are required to transport Lake Park school if there are **673** students and **19** teachers? _____

7) The area of the shaded square is **20cm²**. What is the area of the whole square? _____

8) What is the order of rotational symmetry of this shape? _____

9) What is the highest common factor of **81** and **135**? _____

10) What is the next number in the sequence?
1, 4, 10, 22, _____

11) What is the next number in the sequence?
12, 6, 3, _____, $\frac{3}{4}$

12) A digital clock in Madrid reads **18:32**. New York is **7** hours behind Madrid. What time is it in New York on a 12-hour clock? _____

13) $13^2 - (6^2 + 45) =$ _____

14) In which century was **1525**? _____

15) What is **900mℓ** as a percentage of **4.5ℓ**? _____

Score [ ]   Percentage [%]

Do your workings on this page

Mark to %	
0	0%
1	7%
2	13%
3	20%
4	27%
5	33%
6	40%
7	47%
8	53%
9	60%
10	67%
11	73%
12	80%
13	87%
14	93%
15	100%

Maths Test 21

1) $10^4 - 8^3 =$ _____

2) What is **85%** of **315**? _____

3) **0.35 > 0.355**   Is this true? _____

4) $12^3 + 14^2 =$ _____

5) Increase **155** by **55%**. _____

6) $\frac{y}{8} = 18$

What is the value of **y**? _____

7) Put in size order, largest first:

4.598   4.5   4.599 _____

8) If a negative number is multiplied with another negative number, will the answer be positive or negative? _____

9) A greengrocer sells **25** apples on Saturday and an average of **60** apples on each of the other six days. What is her daily average for the whole week? _____

10) **19%** of people cycle to work, **20.5%** drive to work, **16.75%** walk and the rest take the bus. What percentage travel by bus? _____

11) Change from a % to a fraction:

65% = _____

12) Fill in the missing number:

91, 95, 103, _____ **, 151**

13) $15\overline{)2277} =$ _____
(Write the answer as a decimal.)

14) **Eighteen** is a multiple of **2**. It is also a multiple of **9**.

Which of these numbers are multiples of both **9** and **4**?

_____

36   18   72   60

15) Which triangle contains an obtuse angle? _____

Score [   ]   Percentage [   ] %

Do your workings on this page

Mark to %	
0	0%
1	7%
2	13%
3	20%
4	27%
5	33%
6	40%
7	47%
8	53%
9	60%
10	67%
11	73%
12	80%
13	87%
14	93%
15	100%

Maths Test 22

1) What is the next number in the series?

720, 120, 24, _____

2) $\dfrac{28}{40}$ = _____ %

3) Caroline sat three tests. She scored **84%** in maths, **62%** in English and **76%** in science. What was her mean percentage? _____

4) _____ − $12^2 = 5^2$

5) Express **72** as a product of its prime factors. _____

6) What is the size of angle *x*? _____

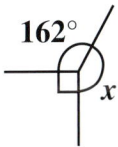

162°

x

7) The supermarket has two brands of cereal. Which cereal brand is better value? _____

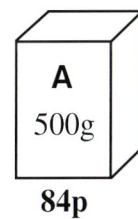

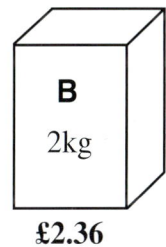

A
500g
84p

B
2kg
£2.36

8) **1** inch ≈ **2.5cm**. How many centimetres are there in a foot? _____

9) **652 × 143 = 93,236**

65.2 × 1.43 = _____

10) What is **24%** of **650**? _____

11) There are three cars on a bridge. The weight limit for the bridge is **3** tonnes. Can a car weighing **830kg** travel along the bridge at the same time as the three cars? _____

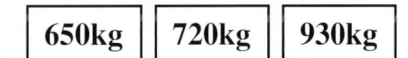

| 650kg | 720kg | 930kg |

12) What fraction of **2km** is **125m**? _____

13) **777 × 7** = _____

14) Ryan recorded the temperature on a winter's day. In the morning it was **7°C**. The temperature dropped by **12°C** throughout the day. What was the temperature at the end of the day? _____

15)

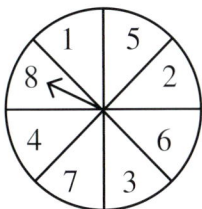

In a game, a player spins a fair spinner and moves the number of spaces the spinner lands on. To win, Oliver needs to score a **6** or higher. What is the probability that Oliver wins on his next turn? _____

Score [ ]　Percentage [%]

Do your workings on this page

Mark to %	
0	0%
1	7%
2	13%
3	20%
4	27%
5	33%
6	40%
7	47%
8	53%
9	60%
10	67%
11	73%
12	80%
13	87%
14	93%
15	100%

Maths Test 23

1) What is **55p** as a % of **£2.50**? _____

2) $14^3 + 15^3 =$ _____

3) What fraction of **one** day is **2** hours and **30** minutes? _____ (Give the answer in lowest terms.)

4) What is the size of angle *a*? _____

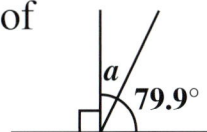

79.9°

5) How many **hundreds** are in $\frac{3}{5}$ of **one million**? _____

6) The average age of four people is **58**. The age of three of these people is **52**. What is the age of the fourth person? _____

7) Which of these is a multiple of **9**? _____

91   19   95   81

8) What is the size of angle *a*? _____

a   116°

9) Put in size order, smallest first:

0.187   18.2% $\frac{5}{27}$

_____

10) Convert this decimal to a %.

2.97 = _____

11) Which of these are common multiples of **15** and **7**? _____

105   30   210   55   98

12) Which fraction is greater than $\frac{1}{5}$ but less than $\frac{7}{8}$? _____

$\frac{1}{6}$ $\frac{9}{25}$ $\frac{15}{16}$ $\frac{6}{35}$

13) **3** out of every **9** children in a class like science. If **18** like science, how many children are there in the class? _____

14) What is the size of angle $\hat{ACB}$? _____

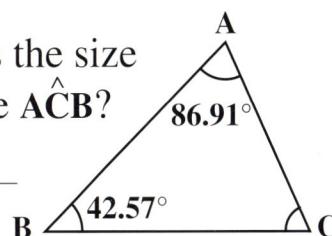

A

86.91°

42.57°

B   C

15) The prime factors of **108** are 2^2 and _____ .

Score [   ]   Percentage [   ] %

Do your workings on this page

Mark to %	
0	0%
1	7%
2	13%
3	20%
4	27%
5	33%
6	40%
7	47%
8	53%
9	60%
10	67%
11	73%
12	80%
13	87%
14	93%
15	100%

Maths Test 24

1) $(7 + 7)^2 - (8^2 + 5^2) \times 3 =$ _____

2) $6^4 \times 4 =$ _____

3) If **20** builders took **4** days to build a house, how long would it take **10** builders? _____

4) $19\overline{)4687} =$ _____
(Write your answer correct to 2 d.p.)

5) Which of these are common multiples of **8** and **14**?

112 28 42 56 224 64 _____

6) The prime factors of **36** are **3²** and _____ .

7) What is the next number in the sequence?
120, **6**, **0.3**, _____

8) What is the difference between the lowest common multiple and the highest common factor of **24**, **12** and **18**? _____

9) One winter's day the temperature was **4°C**. That night it dropped to **-7°C**. How many degrees colder was it that night? _____

10) Two angles of a triangle are **70°** and **40°**.
    a) What is the size of the third angle? _____
    b) What is type of triangle is this? _____

11) When $\frac{5}{6}$ of a certain number is reduced by **21** the result is **119**. What is this number? _____

12) **45%** of **600** entrants turned up to an exam of which only $\frac{1}{3}$ passed. How many passed? _____

13) If a pack of **52** playing cards is shuffled, what is the probability of drawing an odd numbered card? _____

14) **Five** out of every **7** girls in a class like squash. If there are **28** girls in the class, how many girls do not like squash? _____

15) On a farm there are **14** cows, **twice** as many pigs and $\frac{1}{2}$ as many sheep. How many animals are there on the farm? _____

Score [ ] Percentage [%]

Do your workings on this page

Mark to %	
0	0%
1	7%
2	13%
3	20%
4	27%
5	33%
6	40%
7	47%
8	53%
9	60%
10	67%
11	73%
12	80%
13	87%
14	93%
15	100%

Maths Test 25

1) Annie buys **£122.60** worth of clothes. The shop has a sale on, giving customers **10%** off the total cost of their shop when they spend more than **£100**. How much did Annie spend in total? _____

2) Which of these numbers are rectangular? _____

   6   7   11   14   19   23

3) Put these in order, largest first.

   $\frac{3}{5}$ **62%   0.613** _____

4) Solve the following equation:

   $162 = 3 \times \underline{\quad} \times 9$

5) If all columns, rows and diagonals add up to **54**, what are the values of **A** and **B**?

   A = _____

   B = _____

B		A
		18
	2	22

6) Michael has **£234** and Louise has **£126**. Express these amounts in a ratio.

   _____ : _____

7) What is the next number in the sequence?   **1, 1, 2, 3, 5,** ____

8) Abigail thinks of a number. She multiplies it by **6** and subtracts **22**. The answer she gets is **68**. What was her initial number? _____

9) What is **12%** of **350**? _____

10) What is the size of angle *a*? _____

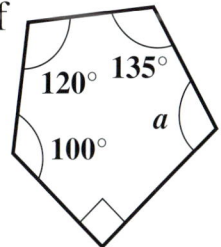

    120° 135°

    a

    100°

11) $\frac{2.8}{0.7} = $ ____

12) $18^2 - 9^2 = $ _____

13) A recycling company offers **6p** for every empty can brought back after use. Joseph brings **17** boxes each containing **23** empty cans. How much will he be given? _____

14) What is the size of angle *y*? _____

    132°

    y

15) What is the next number in the sequence?

    0.0016, 0.016, 0.16, 1.6, _____

Score [ ] Percentage [ ] **%**

Do your workings on this page

Mark to %	
0	0%
1	7%
2	13%
3	20%
4	27%
5	33%
6	40%
7	47%
8	53%
9	60%
10	67%
11	73%
12	80%
13	87%
14	93%
15	100%

Maths Test 26

1) $3.47 \times 0.4 =$ _____

2) Reduce **376** by **75%**. _____

3) What is the highest common factor of **24** and **56**? _____

4) A shopkeeper mixes **60** red marbles and **100** blue marbles with **170** white marbles. If there are **16** marbles in each pack, how many packs can the shopkeeper make? _____

5) What is the **26th** odd number?

_____

6) How many minutes is $\frac{7}{12}$ of a day? _____

7) What is the fewest number of sweet packets that can be arranged in multipacks of either **6**, **9** or **12**? _____

8) All sides of this magic square add up to **69**.

Find the values of **A** and **B**.

24		21
A	23	
	22	B

a) **A =** _____   b) **B =** _____

9) $a = 4$ $b = 5$ $c = 6$

$2a + 4b \times c =$ _____

10) $(0 \times 6) \div 3 =$ _____

11) $17\overline{)8954} =$ _____

(Give your answer to 3 d.p.)

12) What is the missing number?

14, 18, 26, _____ , 54, 74

13) A pet shop has a number of different coloured parrots. The ratio of red to blue to green parrots is **3 : 4 : 5**. If there are **48** parrots in total, how many are not green? _____

14) What is the size of angle x? _____

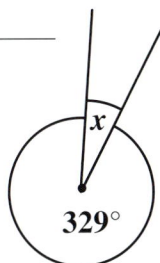

329°

15) On a plan, a park is drawn to a scale of **5cm** to **8m**. If the width of the field is **20m**, what would this measure on the plan? _____

Score [   ]   Percentage [   ] **%**

Do your workings on this page

Mark to %	
0	0%
1	7%
2	13%
3	20%
4	27%
5	33%
6	40%
7	47%
8	53%
9	60%
10	67%
11	73%
12	80%
13	87%
14	93%
15	100%

Maths Test 27

1) Increase **£9.20** by **25%**. _____

2) $1 \div$ _____ $= 0.00001$

3) $x = 7$ $y = 9$

   $x^2 + 5y + y^3 =$ _____

4) The prime factors of a number are 2^4 and 3^5. What is the number? _____

5) The temperature in Antarctica is **-20**°C. The temperature in Cromer is **5**°C. What is the temperature difference? _____

6) Take **five hundred and sixty two thousand** from **three million, four hundred and twenty thousand**. _____

7) $17\overline{)6572} =$ _____

   Give your answer to 2 d.p.

8) Through how many degrees does the minute hand of a clock turn from **8.57pm** to **9.49pm**? _____

9) There are **19** rows of **26** seats on each side of a football stadium. What is the total number of seats on all four sides of the ground? _____

10) Which of these letters have perpendicular lines? _____

    F A E Z S

11) Write the shaded sector **A** as a fraction of a full rotation. _____

12) What is the lowest common multiple (LCM) of **8**, **16** and **12**? _____

13) What is the highest common factor of **81**, **54** and **144**? _____

14) In a large bag of marbles there are **16** green marbles, **three** times as many red marbles and **seven** times as many yellow marbles. How many marbles are there in the bag? _____

15) The middle number of **9** consecutive even numbers is **100**. What is the **eighth** number in this series? _____

Score [   ]   Percentage [%]

Do your workings on this page

Mark to %	
0	0%
1	7%
2	13%
3	20%
4	27%
5	33%
6	40%
7	47%
8	53%
9	60%
10	67%
11	73%
12	80%
13	87%
14	93%
15	100%

Maths Test 28

1) $15^4 =$ _____

2) $a = 7 \quad b = 8 \quad c = 15$

$5a + 6b - 2c =$ _____

3) What is $\frac{1}{5}$ of $\frac{1}{7}$? _____

4) What is the size of angle y? _____

108° y

5) $21 \overline{)}$ $\quad$ **8r 12**

Fill in the missing number.

6) Reduce **950** by **38%**. _____

7) $23^2 =$ _____

8) What is the size of angle a? _____

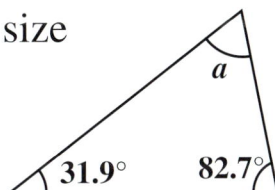

a

31.9° $\quad$ 82.7°

9) $84 \overline{)4624} =$ _____

(Give your answer as a decimal to 2 d.p.)

10) What is the size of angle b? _____

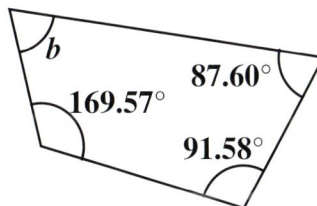

b

169.57° $\quad$ 87.60°

91.58°

11) An aeroplane holds **115** people. If **567** people book to fly from London to Paris, how many aeroplanes will be needed? _____

12) Aman scored **49** out of **70** in a test. What percentage did he achieve? _____

13) What is this shape? _____

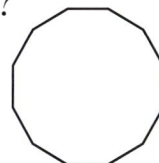

14) What is the highest common factor of **78**, **130** and **195**? _____

15) What is **645** grams as a % of **5.5kg**? _____
(Give your answer to 2 d.p.)

Score ☐ Percentage ☐ %

Do your workings on this page

Mark to %	
0	0%
1	7%
2	13%
3	20%
4	27%
5	33%
6	40%
7	47%
8	53%
9	60%
10	67%
11	73%
12	80%
13	87%
14	93%
15	100%

Maths Test 29

1) What is the next number in this sequence?

    7, 8, 9, 12, 11, 16, ____

2) A clock loses **3** seconds every minute. How many minutes will it lose in **2** days? ____

3) Sweets were shared out between Bhilhan and Max in the ratio **3 : 7**. If Bhilhan received **12** sweets, how many did Max receive? ____

4) Pavandeep and Kim share out some money between them in the ratio **8 : 6**. If Kim was given **£8.40**, how much did Pavandeep receive?

    _____

5) $a = 5$ $b = 6$ $c = 7$

    $4c + 6b - 3a =$ ____

6) What is the LCM of **4**, **9** and **12**? ____

7) Ben took a survey of the colour of houses on his street. Out of the **200** buildings, **20%** were brown, $\frac{1}{4}$ were black and **10** houses were green. The rest were red. How many houses were red? ____

8) Harveer scored **19** out of **25** in his maths test. What percentage did he get? ____

9) **84** children in a school go home for lunch. **25%** do not. How many children in total are there in the school? ____

10) Which of these is an isosceles triangle? ____

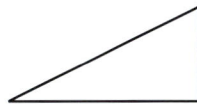

A   B   C   D

11) What is the average of **66**, **132** and **153**? ____

12) $13\overline{)2342}$ = ____

    (Give your answer to 1 d.p.)

13) What is $\frac{1}{3}$ of $\frac{3}{8}$? ____

14) What is the size of angle **a**? ____

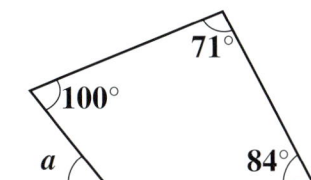

15) Which two consecutive square numbers have a difference of **17**? ____

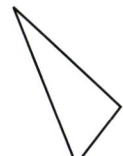

Score ☐ Percentage ☐ **%**

Do your workings on this page

Mark to %	
0	0%
1	7%
2	13%
3	20%
4	27%
5	33%
6	40%
7	47%
8	53%
9	60%
10	67%
11	73%
12	80%
13	87%
14	93%
15	100%

Maths Test 30

1) What is the sum of all the interior angles of this shape? _____

2) What is **84p** as a percentage of **£1.40**? _____

3) $18^2 =$ _____

4) What is the missing number? _____

$$21\overline{)\ ?}\quad 5\ \text{r}12$$

5) $100 - 28 = 6 \times$ _____

6) **40% of 85 =** _____

7) What is the size of angle **a**? _____

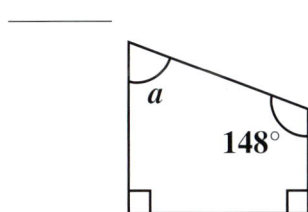

8) What is the missing number?

   2.65, 2.7, 2.74, ____, 2.79, 2.8

9) What is the largest possible remainder when dividing by **18**? _____

10) In **four** years' time, Victoria will be $3\frac{1}{2}$ times older than her brother. If she is currently **31**, how old is her brother now? _____

11) Which shape has a different perimeter from the others? _____

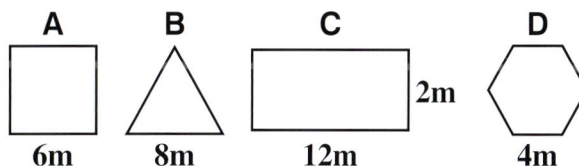

A □ 6m   B △ 8m   C ▭ 12m 2m   D ⬡ 4m

12) The temperature is **-19°C**. What will it be if it rises by **17°C**? _____

13) What is $\frac{1}{2}$ of $\frac{1}{8}$? _____

14) There are **5** minutes of advertising after every **20** minutes of television time. If this pattern were consistent for every hour, what fraction of an hour would be used for advertising? _____

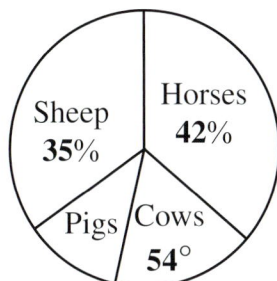

15) What is the size of the angle represented by pigs? _____

Sheep 35%
Horses 42%
Pigs
Cows 54°

Score [ ]   Percentage [%]

Do your workings on this page

Mark to %	
0	0%
1	7%
2	13%
3	20%
4	27%
5	33%
6	40%
7	47%
8	53%
9	60%
10	67%
11	73%
12	80%
13	87%
14	93%
15	100%

Maths Test 31

1) $2.5^2 =$ _____

2) Write **17:56** using **am** or **pm**. _____

3) What is the size of angle **a**? _____

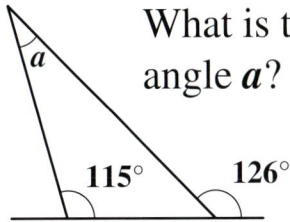

115°   126°

4) What is the size of angle A$\hat{B}$C? _____

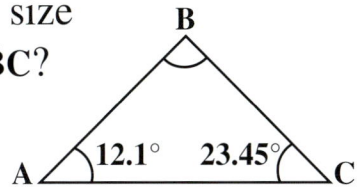

B   12.1°   23.45°   A   C

5) What number is halfway between **-8** and **+4**? _____

6) $23\overline{)5864} =$ _____ (Give your answer to 2 d.p.)

7) The average age of three people is **45**. If one is **20** and another is **56**, how old is the third person? _____

8) Jim scored **29** out of **75** in a maths test. What percentage did he achieve? (Give your answer to 2 d.p.) _____

9) 5^3 is a prime factor of **875**. What is the other prime factor? _____

10) A multiple of **13** is any number that has **13** as a factor. Which is not a multiple of **13**? _____
65   117   26   186   338

11) What fraction of a day is **5** hours and **20** minutes? Write the fraction in its lowest terms. _____

12) What is the missing number?   **9072, 1512, 252,** _____ **, 7**

13) Mr Singh takes an aeroplane from Delhi to London. The flight takes **8** hours and **53** minutes. If Mr Singh leaves at **8.51am** (London time), at what time will he arrive in London? _____

14) What is the smallest number that can be divided by **500, 600** and **1,000**? _____

15) What is the highest common factor of **27, 36** and **45**? _____

Score [ ]   Percentage [ ] %

Do your workings on this page

Mark to %	
0	0%
1	7%
2	13%
3	20%
4	27%
5	33%
6	40%
7	47%
8	53%
9	60%
10	67%
11	73%
12	80%
13	87%
14	93%
15	100%

Maths Test 32

1) $(13^2 + 4^2) \times 2^3 =$ _____

2) $24.2 \times 0.89 =$ _____

3) Louise ran a **100m** race in **13.27** seconds and Anisha ran it in **12.53** seconds. How many seconds faster was Anisha? _____

4) Complete this number sequence:

$1\frac{1}{2}$, $2\frac{1}{4}$, **3**, _____

5) $x = 7$ $y = 5$ $z = 3$

$\dfrac{x + y}{z} =$ _____

6) What is the highest common factor of **46**, **69** and **115**? _____

7) What is the next number?

0.0015, 0.015, 0.15, _____

8) Find the size of angle z. _____

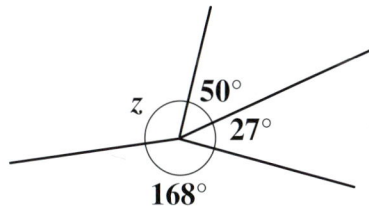

9) $8^3 =$ _____

10) Helen is the middle person in a row of students. She is also **11th** from the end. How many students are there in the whole row? _____

11) Sweets are shared between Michael and Molly in the ratio **8 : 5**. Molly receives the smaller share of **15** sweets.
a) How many sweets does Michael receive? _____
b) How many sweets are there altogether? _____

12) Find the sum of the prime numbers between **38** and **58**. _____

13) $7^4 =$ _____

14) A local theatre has **8** seats in each of the **4** boxes, **20** rows of **21** seats in the circle and **14** rows of **10** seats in the stalls. How many seats are there altogether? _____

15) 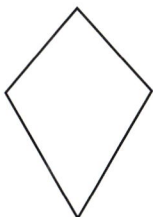 What is this quadrilateral called?

_____

Score [ ] Percentage [%]

Do your workings on this page

Mark to %	
0	0%
1	7%
2	13%
3	20%
4	27%
5	33%
6	40%
7	47%
8	53%
9	60%
10	67%
11	73%
12	80%
13	87%
14	93%
15	100%

Maths Test 33

1) What is the **8th** rectangular number? _____

2) $4.9 \div 1.96 =$ _____

3) The prime factors of a number are **11** and 3^4. What is the number? _____

4) $18^3 + 19^2 =$ _____

5) Write in size order, starting with the biggest.

   -15 5 -10 7 15 -6

   _____

6) Write in size order, starting with the smallest.

   $\frac{20}{100}$ $\frac{1}{20}$ **21%** _____

7) What is the size of angle **b**? _____

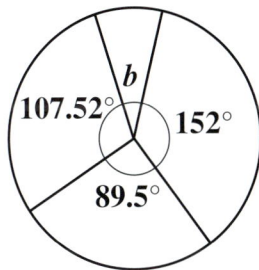

   107.52° b 152° 89.5°

8) What fraction of this circle is shaded?

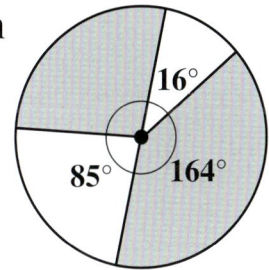

   16° 85° 164°

   _____

9) $\frac{1}{4} + \frac{1}{12} + \frac{15}{48} =$ _____

10) This is a clock in a mirror. What is the time? _____ am

11) What is the size of angle **a**?

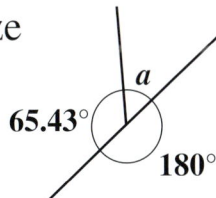

   _____

   65.43° a 180°

12) What is the lowest common multiple (LCM) of **8**, **12** and **6**? _____

13) Find the highest common factor (HCF) of **320**, **128** and **256**. _____

14) $28 \overline{)7548} =$ _____   (Give the answer to 2 d.p.)

15)

A	7	
	5	B
	3	8

This magic square adds up to the same amount in all directions. What are the values of **A** and **B**?

A = _____

B = _____

Score [   ]   Percentage [   ] %

Do your workings on this page

© 2016 Stephen Curran

Mark to %	
0	0%
1	7%
2	13%
3	20%
4	27%
5	33%
6	40%
7	47%
8	53%
9	60%
10	67%
11	73%
12	80%
13	87%
14	93%
15	100%

Maths Test 34

1) How many faces does a cube have? _____

2) $12 \div 0.3 =$ _____

3) Which of these numbers is both a square and cube number? _____

1 8 9 16 36

4) Put in size order, starting with the smallest.

$\dfrac{2}{3}$ $\dfrac{1}{2}$ 45% $\dfrac{5}{6}$ 0.85

_____

5) Is a square-based pyramid a prism? _____

6) **220** children in a school like maths, **12%** do not. How many children are there in the school? _____

7) The average age of three girls is **16** years. One girl is **21** years old and the second is **12** years old. How old is the third girl? _____

8) How many sides does a nonagon have? _____

9) $\dfrac{1}{16} \times 4 =$ _____

10) What fraction of the circle is shaded? _____

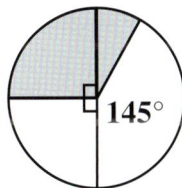

11) A crate can hold **32** bottles. If Henry needs **390** bottles, how many crates should he buy? _____

12) What is the average of **12**, **14** and **21**? _____ (Give your answer to 2 d.p.)

13) $13\overline{)2078} =$ _____ (Give your answer to 2 d.p.)

14) Claire's watch is **7** minutes slow. At what time (on her watch) must she start her **12** minute journey to school if she wants to be there at **8.10am**? _____

15) What is the size of angle **a**? _____

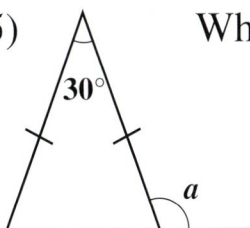

Do your workings on this page

Mark to %	
0	0%
1	7%
2	13%
3	20%
4	27%
5	33%
6	40%
7	47%
8	53%
9	60%
10	67%
11	73%
12	80%
13	87%
14	93%
15	100%

Maths Test 35

1) What is the next number in the sequence?

 2, 1, $\frac{1}{2}$, $\frac{1}{4}$, _____

2) $x = 4$ $y = 8$

 $y^2 \div x =$ _____

3) A plan of a school hall measures **9cm** by **12cm**. If the actual width of the hall measures **13.5m**, what is the actual length of the hall? _____

4) **3³** is a prime factor of **81**. What is the other prime factor? _____

5) Mary wrote the answer to a mathematics question as **2.15** instead of the correct answer of **21.5**. What was the difference between Mary's answer and the correct answer? _____

6) What is the HCF of **32**, **48** and **64**? _____

7) Complete this number sequence:

 3, 6, 9, 15, 24, 39, _____, _____

8) $4^3 + 2^4 + 17^2 =$ _____

9) **69.1 ÷ 0.12 =** _____
 (Give your answer to 2 d.p.)

10) Write **sixteen minutes before midnight** in 24-hour clock. _____

11) What is the size of angle **a**? _____

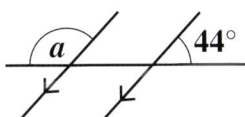

12) What is the size of angle **b**? _____

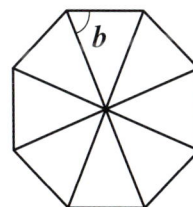

13) Which shape has the most lines of symmetry? _____

 A B C

14) How many matches in total will there be between **four** badminton players if they all play each other once? _____

15) This magic square adds up to the same amount in all directions. What are the values of **A** and **B**?

A	9	
	13	B
12	17	

 A = _____

 B = _____

 Score [ ] Percentage [ ] %

Do your workings on this page

Mark to %	
0	0%
1	7%
2	13%
3	20%
4	27%
5	33%
6	40%
7	47%
8	53%
9	60%
10	67%
11	73%
12	80%
13	87%
14	93%
15	100%

Maths Test 36

1) $14.26 \div 2.5 =$ _____

2) $12 \times$ _____ $\times 9 = 1{,}620$

3) What is the lowest common multiple (LCM) of **7**, **8** and **14**? _____

4) What number is halfway between **-9** and **+7**? _____

5) What is the size of angle a? _____

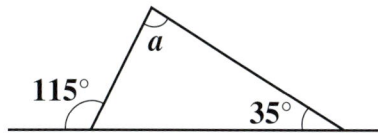

6) What is the highest common factor of **64**, **72** and **96**? _____

7) $\dfrac{4}{5} + \dfrac{3}{20} =$ _____

8) A clock chimes **4** times every **20** minutes. How many times does it chime in one day? _____

9) How does the time **15 minutes after midnight** appear on a 24-hour clock? _____

10) Subtract the sum of the odd numbers between **56** and **66** from **500**. _____

11) What is the product of the prime numbers between **92** and **102**? _____

12) What is the next number in the sequence?

1, 3, 7, 15, _____

13) $2.4^3 =$ _____

14) The average amount of money spent by six girls on a shopping trip was **£29**. If the average amount spent by five of the girls was **£30**, how much did the sixth girl spend? _____

15) 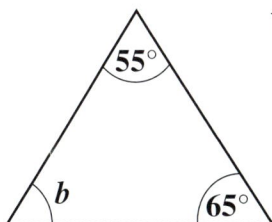 What is the size of angle b? _____

Score [ ] Percentage [ ] %

Do your workings on this page

Mark to %	
0	0%
1	7%
2	13%
3	20%
4	27%
5	33%
6	40%
7	47%
8	53%
9	60%
10	67%
11	73%
12	80%
13	87%
14	93%
15	100%

Maths Test 37

1) $0.0807 \times 10^3 =$ _____

2) What is the area of this triangle? _____
(Round to 1 d.p.)
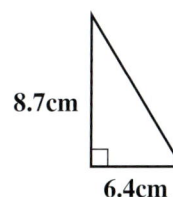
8.7cm
6.4cm

3) A woman is exactly **44** years old. Her son is $\frac{1}{3}$ of her age. What age is her son in years and months? _____

4) $\frac{1.4}{0.007} =$ _____

5) Complete this sequence:
75, 15, 25, 5, 15, ____ , ____

6) $1\frac{3}{8} - \frac{16}{28} =$ _____

7) All directions add up to **102**.

A = _____

B = _____

28		B
44	34	
	A	

8) What is the reflex angle made by the hands of this clock? _____
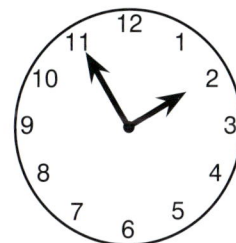

9) Out of **150** children taking a English exam, **70%** passed. Out of those who passed, $\frac{1}{15}$ got full marks. How many children got full marks? _____

10) When a number is cubed and then multiplied by **7** the answer is **189**. What is the number? _____

11) $\frac{5}{9}$ of the children in a drama club are boys. **76** are girls. How many children are there altogether in the club? _____

12) How many faces does a pentagonal-based pyramid have? _____

13) $3\frac{11}{15} \div \frac{8}{9} =$ _____
(Simplify fully.)

14) There are **6** hockey teams and each team plays each other once. How many games will be played? _____

15) What is the order of rotational symmetry of this shape? _____

Score [ ] Percentage [ ] %

Do your workings on this page

Mark to %	
0	0%
1	7%
2	13%
3	20%
4	27%
5	33%
6	40%
7	47%
8	53%
9	60%
10	67%
11	73%
12	80%
13	87%
14	93%
15	100%

Maths Test 38

1) Complete this sequence:

1, 2, 10, 37, _____

2) What is the value of y? ____

$4(7y - 12) = 176$

3) When three consecutive numbers are added together the total is **39**. Find these three numbers. _____

4) How many lines of symmetry does a kite have? _____

5) What is the area of this parallelogram?

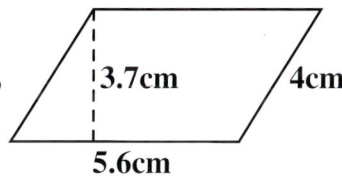

_____

3.7cm   **4cm**

5.6cm

6) $2\frac{3}{8} \times 2\frac{4}{19} =$ _____

7) ____ $\div$ **2,000 = 0.04**

8) Find the height of this triangle when the area is **192cm²**. _____

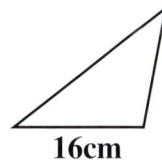

16cm

9) $\dfrac{0.175}{1.4 \times 0.02} =$ ____

10) $13 - (6 \times 4\frac{2}{3}) =$ ____

11) A watch loses **3** minutes every hour. At what time on what day will the watch be exactly **2** hours behind if the watch was put right at **6pm** on a Wednesday? _____

12) Plot the co-ordinates and join them up.

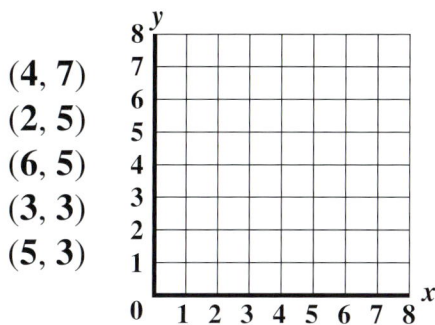

(4, 7)
(2, 5)
(6, 5)
(3, 3)
(5, 3)

What shape is this?

_____

13) The area of the triangle is **24cm²** with a height of **4cm**. What is the area of the circle using Area = πr^2 (π = **3.14**)? _____

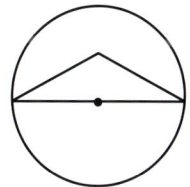

14) **1 7 7 5 4 6 2 1 1**

What is the:

a) range? ____   b) mode? ____

c) median? ____

15)

a **117°**

143°

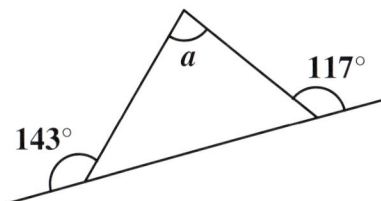

What is the size of angle a? _____

Score ____   Percentage ____ %

Do your workings on this page

Mark to %	
0	0%
1	7%
2	13%
3	20%
4	27%
5	33%
6	40%
7	47%
8	53%
9	60%
10	67%
11	73%
12	80%
13	87%
14	93%
15	100%

Maths Test 39

1) Which is the odd one out? _____
   cuboid   cube   kite   triangular prism

2) An aeroplane leaves London at **14:30** (London time) on Tuesday and arrives at Moscow at **06:10** (Moscow time) on Wednesday. How long was the journey if Moscow is **8** hours ahead of London? _____

3) If there is **360°** in a full circle, what fraction is **108°** of a semi-circle? _____

4) What are the next two numbers in this sequence?
   96, 95, 91, 82, 66, ___, ___

5) What is the sum of the odd numbers between **38** and **54**? _____

6) A seat at a theatre show costs **£12.50** and there are **30** rows of **10** seats each side of the centre aisle. How much money will one show make if all the seats are sold? _____

7) $4^3 + 5^3 + 6^2 =$ _____^{2}

8) Use the conversion graph to find the following distances:
   a) **35** miles = _____ km
   b) **16km** = _____ miles

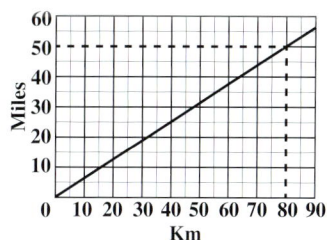

9) What is the highest common factor of **42**, **90** and **144**? _____

10) $2^6 = 2 \times 2 \times 2 \times 2 \times 2 \times 2 = 64$

    $2^8 \times 3^2 =$ _____

11) What is the volume of this cuboid?
    8cm   13cm   6cm
    _____

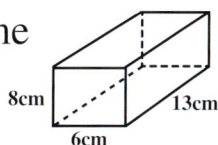

12) The sum of two numbers is **75**. Their difference is **9**. What are the two numbers? _____

13) The area of half a tennis court is **2,808ft²**. If the width of the court is **36ft**, what is the length of the full court? _____

14) How many degrees are there in **12** right angles? _____

15) Write **1.012%** as a decimal. _____

Score _____   Percentage _____%

Do your workings on this page

Mark to %	
0	0%
1	7%
2	13%
3	20%
4	27%
5	33%
6	40%
7	47%
8	53%
9	60%
10	67%
11	73%
12	80%
13	87%
14	93%
15	100%

Maths Test 40

1) What is the missing mixed number in this sequence?

$$4\frac{1}{8}, \ 4\frac{1}{4}, \ \underline{\hspace{1cm}}, \ 4\frac{1}{2}$$

2) What is the lowest common multiple of **6**, **9** and **15**? _____

3) How many less than **one million** is **869,437**? _____

4) Fatima took **9** books off a shelf and Mark took another **3** books off the same shelf. If **25%** of the books had been removed, how many books were there originally? _____

5) $\frac{7}{9}x = 63$

Find the value of **x**. _____

6) $7t + 9 = 33 - 5t$

Find the value of **t**. _____

7) $3\frac{5}{6} + 1\frac{9}{17} =$ _____

8) What is the value of **A**?

_____

A		0.6
	1.3	1.6
2		

9) Write the ratio **36 : 24** in its lowest terms? _____

10) Add the sum of **13** and **14** to the difference between the square of **13** and **14** and the product of **13** and **14**. _____

11) Find the missing number:

_____ $\longrightarrow \boxed{\times \ 12 + 17} \longrightarrow$ **281**

12) What is the area of a square with a perimeter of **22cm**? _____

13) How many degrees is the clockwise turn from north-east to north? _____

14) Milk condenses at **46°F** and boils at **232°F**. What is the temperature difference between these values? _____

15)

No. of cars (150, 100, 50) — Time (9-12, 12-3, 3-6, 6-9)

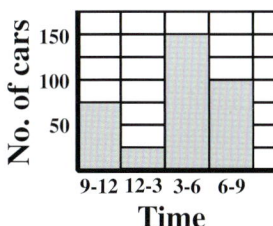

The bar chart shows the number of cars passing a school at various times throughout the day.

a) How many cars passed altogether? _____

b) What is the range? _____

Score [ ] Percentage [ ] %

Notes

Answers

Test 1
1) 4
2) 6.09
3) 360
4) 23
5) 25
6) horizontal
7) 16
8) 34
9) 1, 2, 3, 4, 6, 8, 12, 24
10) 3.5
11) D
12) B
13) 10 days 16 hours
14) 1.45
15) 69

Test 2
1) 10
2) 5
3) no
4) $^1/_{54}$
5) 1, 2, 3, 4, 6, 8, 12, 16, 24, 48
6) 22
7) 540°
8) 19
9) 20
10) 0.96
11) 124
12) Amber
13) 3
14) $^1/_3$
15) 72

Test 3
1) 385
2) 28
3) 7 thousandths or 0.007 or $^7/_{1000}$
4) Shereen
5) -5.4

6) 50
7) Yes
8) 43
9) 5.473
10) 17.4
11) 5 : 8
12) 2 : 1
13) 7 : 6
14) 8.31am
15) 13

Test 4
1) 20
2) 3
3) E
4) B
5) 12
6) 1928
7) 5
8) 22.5°
9) :::::
10) 4
11) 5.96
12) 96
13) 18p
14) 0.58
15) 55

Test 5
1) 304
2) 38, 45
3) C
4) 7
5) 11
6) 12
7) 0.03
8) No
9) 75
10) $^7/_{1000}$
11) 2
12) 336
13) 7
14) D
15) 10,080

Test 6
1) 25
2) 1.975
3) 726
4) 1924
5) A = 21, B = 23
6) $^1/_8$
7) 1, 2, 3, 4, 6, 9, 12, 18, 36
8) 30
9) 28
10) 0.15
11) 4,200
12) 18
13) 9
14) Tuesday
15) 35

Test 7
1) 27.8496
2) 55
3) 237°
4) 2,825.7
5) 92
6) 7 hundredths or 0.07 or $^7/_{100}$
7) $6^4/_5$, $6^5/_6$, 6.85
8) 263.8
9) $^1/_6$
10) 7 : 9
11) 3.43pm
12) 8,170
13) 11
14) 68
15) 11.35pm

Test 8
1) 25
2) 0.64
3) 01/01/2014
4) 32
5) 1, 2, 4, 7, 14, 28
6) 10

7) 13
8) 36
9) 18
10) 1, 2, 3, 6
11) 19,992
12) 5
13) 22
14) B
15) A

Test 9
1) 6.5 or $6^1/_2$
2) 926.972
3) 144, 49
4) 27
5) 22.5
6) 4
7) 26
8) 72, 30
9) 90
10) 5 : 3 : 6
11) 8
12) 2,179
13) 0.68
14) 15
15) $^2/_3$

Test 10
1) 144, 64
2) 5
3) 7.125, 7.12, $7^1/_9$
4) -2
5) 13
6) 12
7) 207
8) 55 hours 30mins
9) 1.9668
10) $^4/_{13}$
11) 9.13%, 0.915, $^{914}/_{100}$
12) 179°
13) 8

Answers

14) parallel
15) 9.10am

Test 11
1) 1, 29
2) 6
3) 39, 195
4) 18
5) $^{41}/_{60}$
6) 34
7) 49
8) No
9) 0.54
10) 38, 102, 51, 91
11) Increase
12) 16
13) 165
14) 233
15) A & C

Test 12
1) 50,000
2) 1,728
3) 2,185
4) 11, 32
5) 26
6) 568
7) $^{9}/_{20}$
8) $^{167}/_{18}$
9) $^{17}/_{19}$
10) 2042
11) d
12) Infinite or ∞
13) 7 tenths, 0.7 or $^{7}/_{10}$
14) 60
15) 11.19am

Test 13
1) 901.5
2) $^{1}/_{5}$
3) 4.8
4) 1, 3, 7, 21
5) 1978

6) 57
7) 97
8) 4
9) 28, 36
10) 38, 63
11) 1
12) 16
13) 27
14) $^{1}/_{3}$
15) 6 thousandths or 0.006 or $^{6}/_{1000}$

Test 14
1) 9, 56, 168
2) 5.00
3) $^{9}/_{20}$
4) a) 73m
   b) 208m^2
5) 569
6) 87
7) 15
8) B
9) 0.65
10) 10:10
11) $^{4}/_{9}$
12) 175
13) 449
14) 1464
15) –

Test 15
1) 126°
2) 36cm^3
3) 40%
4) 28°C
5) a) 800 b) 250
6) A = 25, B = 24
7) 38, 52
8) 540°
9) 13
10) 0.0001
11) 180
12) 10

13) 29.75
14) 15
15) $^{7}/_{24}$

Test 16
1) $^{3}/_{8}$
2) 1,000,000
3) 6.9
4) $^{109}/_{200}$
5) 60%
6) 379.42
7) $1^{1}/_{30}$
8) 29
9) 43
10) 9.33am
11) South
12) radius
13) $^{23}/_{48}$
14) Two from: 2, 3, 4, 6, 12
15) £21

Test 17
1) North
2) 14
3) $^{2}/_{45}$
4) £13.50
5) 69
6) 43
7) 102
8) $^{22}/_{45}$
9) 45 and 36
10) 459.90
11) 8.10am
12) 0.18
13) 3
14) 368
15) $^{1}/_{20}$

Test 18
1) c
2) £2.85
3) 7.33am
4) 60
5) 9

6) 84
7) parallelogram
8) 729
9) $^{1}/_{12}$
10) 3
11) 6cm
12) 135
13) 14
14) 13
15) 12

Test 19
1) 17
2) 270mℓ
3) 106°
4) 16m
5) 12
6) 21:09
7) A & B
8) 6
9) £621.60
10) 4
11) 5 days
12) 7
13) a) 12cm^2
    b) 22cm
14) 46
15) 520

Test 20
1) 150°
2) Tuesday
3) 28
4) 3km
5) 5
6) 14
7) 320cm^2
8) 4
9) 27
10) 46
11) 1.5 or $1^{1}/_{2}$
12) 11.32am
13) 88
14) 16th
15) 20%

Answers

Test 21
1) 9,488
2) 267.75
3) No
4) 1,924
5) 240.25
6) 144
7) 4.599, 4.598, 4.5
8) Positive
9) 55
10) 43.75%
11) $^{13}/_{20}$
12) 119
13) 151.8
14) 36, 72
15) B

Test 22
1) 6
2) 70%
3) 74%
4) 169 or 13^2
5) $2^3 \times 3^2$ or $2 \times 2 \times 2 \times 3 \times 3$
6) 108°
7) B
8) 30cm
9) 93.236
10) 156
11) No
12) $^1/_{16}$
13) 5,439
14) -5°C
15) $^3/_8$

Test 23
1) 22%
2) 6,119
3) $^5/_{48}$
4) 10.1°
5) 6,000
6) 76
7) 81
8) 244°
9) 18.2%, $^5/_{27}$, 0.187
10) 297%
11) 105, 210
12) $^9/_{25}$
13) 54
14) 50.52°
15) 3^3

Test 24
1) -71
2) 5,184
3) 8 days
4) 246.68
5) 112, 56, 224
6) 2^2
7) 0.015
8) 138
9) 11°C
10) a) 70°
    b) Isosceles
11) 168
12) 90
13) $^4/_{13}$
14) 8
15) 49

Test 25
1) £110.34
2) 6, 14
3) 62%, 0.613, $^3/_5$
4) 6
5) A = 6, B = 14
6) 13 : 7
7) 8
8) 15
9) 42
10) 95°
11) 4
12) 243
13) £23.46
14) 42°
15) 16

Test 26
1) 1.388
2) 94
3) 8
4) 20
5) 51
6) 840
7) 36
8) A = 20, B = 22
9) 128
10) 0
11) 526.706
12) 38
13) 28
14) 31°
15) 12.5cm

Test 27
1) £11.50
2) 100,000
3) 823
4) 3,888
5) 25°C
6) 2,858,000
7) 386.59
8) 312°
9) 1,976
10) F, E
11) $^{13}/_{72}$
12) 48
13) 9
14) 176
15) 106

Test 28
1) 50,625
2) 53
3) $^1/_{35}$
4) 72°
5) 180
6) 589
7) 529
8) 65.4°
9) 55.05
10) 11.25°
11) 5
12) 70%
13) Dodecagon
14) 13
15) 11.73%

Test 29
1) 13
2) 144
3) 28
4) £11.20
5) 49
6) 36
7) 100
8) 76%
9) 112
10) B
11) 117
12) 180.2
13) $^1/_8$
14) 75°
15) 64 and 81

Test 30
1) 720°
2) 60%
3) 324
4) 117
5) 12
6) 34
7) 32°
8) 2.77
9) 17
10) 6
11) C
12) -2°C
13) $^1/_{16}$
14) $^1/_4$
15) 28.8°

Test 31
1) 6.25
2) 5.56pm
3) 11°

Answers

4) 144.45°
5) -2
6) 254.96
7) 59
8) 38.67%
9) 7
10) 186
11) $^2/_9$
12) 42
13) 17:44 or 5.44pm
14) 3,000
15) 9

Test 32
1) 1,480
2) 21.538
3) 0.74
4) $3^3/_4$
5) 4
6) 23
7) 1.5
8) 115°
9) 512
10) 21
11) a) 24 b) 39
12) 184
13) 2,401
14) 592
15) Kite

Test 33
1) 15
2) 2.5
3) 891
4) 6,193
5) 15, 7, 5, -6, -10, -15
6) $^1/_{20}$, $^{20}/_{100}$, 21%
7) 10.98°
8) $^{259}/_{360}$
9) $^{31}/_{48}$
10) 4.55am
11) 114.57°

12) 24
13) 64
14) 269.57
15) A = 2, B = 1

Test 34
1) 6
2) 40
3) 1
4) 45%, $^1/_2$, $^2/_3$, $^5/_6$, 0.85
5) No
6) 250
7) 15
8) 9
9) $^1/_4$
10) $^{25}/_{72}$
11) 13
12) 15.67
13) 159.85
14) 7.51am
15) 105°

Test 35
1) $^1/_8$
2) 16
3) 18m
4) 3
5) 19.35
6) 16
7) 63, 102
8) 369
9) 575.83
10) 23:44
11) 136°
12) 67.5°
13) C
14) 6
15) A = 16, B = 15

Test 36
1) 5.704
2) 15
3) 56

4) -1
5) 80°
6) 8
7) $^{19}/_{20}$
8) 288
9) 00:15
10) 195
11) 9,797
12) 31
13) 13.824
14) £24
15) 60°

Test 37
1) 80.7
2) 27.8cm^2
3) 14 years 8 months
4) 200
5) 3, 13
6) $^{45}/_{56}$
7) A = 32, B = 38
8) 270°
9) 7
10) 3
11) 171
12) 6
13) $4^1/_5$
14) 15
15) 8

Test 38
1) 101
2) 8
3) 12, 13, 14
4) 1
5) 20.72cm^2
6) $5^1/_4$
7) 80
8) 24cm
9) 6.25
10) -15
11) 10.00am on Friday

12) Irregular Pentagon
13) 113.04cm^2
14) a) 6 b) 1 c) 4
15) 80°

Test 39
1) Kite
2) 7hrs 40mins
3) $^3/_5$
4) 41, 5
5) 368
6) £7,500
7) 15^2
8) a) 55km
   b) 10 miles
9) 6
10) 2,304
11) 624cm^3
12) 33, 42
13) 156ft
14) 1,080°
15) 0.01012

Test 40
1) $4^3/_8$
2) 90
3) 130,563
4) 48
5) 81
6) 2
7) $5^{37}/_{102}$
8) 0.9
9) 3 : 2
10) 236
11) 22
12) 30.25cm^2
13) 315°
14) 186°F
15) a) 350
    b) 125

PROGRESS CHARTS

Test	Score	%
1		
2		
3		
4		
5		
6		
7		
8		
9		
10		
11		
12		
13		
14		
15		
16		
17		
18		
19		
20		

Test	Score	%
21		
22		
23		
24		
25		
26		
27		
28		
29		
30		
31		
32		
33		
34		
35		
36		
37		
38		
39		
40		

CERTIFICATE OF

ACHIEVEMENT

This certifies

_____

has successfully completed

11+ Maths
Year 5–7
TESTBOOK **2**

Overall percentage
score achieved

%

Comment _____

_____

Signed _____
(teacher/parent/guardian)

Date _____